HOW TO SELL ON ETSY

ETSY SHOP SECRETS TO SELL YOUR CRAFT ONLINE

MONEY MAKER PUBLISHING

CONTENTS

INTRODUCTION

Recently, crafts and homemade goods have gained widespread appeal for customers around the world. The advent of e-commerce has given everyone the opportunity to buy and sell these kinds of products with less effort and red tape. As a result, it's now so much easier to search for and buy the right tools to start their own business because people can now do it from the comfort of their own living room.

The craft market in particular has been booming due to new trading platforms. Homemade crafts may not command the same wow-factor as mainstream manufacturing or the tech industry do, but these products get a huge amount of attention from the public at large. Moreover, that market has only been growing in recent years and by most projections, is expected to keep rising. The Craft and Hobby Association claims that in the United States alone, the crafts industry is worth billions in sales and among these earnings, a large slice came via the online marketplaces.

This is where Etsy comes into play. Although Etsy only started operations 13 years ago, the number of individuals who have established trade deals through the platform as of the end of 2018 is already well over 2 million, and it is expected to keep on rising.

All of this means that Etsy is a great place for someone with the right product to come in and sell their crafts online. If you have a good craft, then there are millions of customers waiting to find it. Of course, there are certain obstacles for a great deal of Etsy sellers, particularly those who have yet to create a steady stream of clientele. And since Etsy commands so much internet traffic, it has become a main destination for sellers of a wide range of crafts and vintage goods. As a result, there will always be competition, and the principle of "survival of the fittest" starts to emerge in the handicraft market. It can be difficult to make your own place on Etsy because it's always a challenge to compete with established merchants. Despite this, with the right plan, product, and training, someone with little prior experience can steadily cultivate a specialty and garner a large equity stake in the crafts industry via the Etsy platform.

1. UNDERSTANDING ETSY

In the simplest terms, Etsy is an online marketplace where people buy and sell different products related to handicrafts and vintage items. If you are in the market for arts and crafts, crafting materials, housewares, paper goods, jewelry, small cosmetic companies, artisan foods, personal care, and apparel, Etsy will be a fantastic site to shop.

At the same time, Etsy is a great place for craft creators as well. The site is a great marketplace where you can try your hand at selling handmade arts and crafts, among other things. If you want to sell old toys, books, games, kitchenware, accessories, jewelry, pictures, clothing, and costumes, then you can start doing it with ease! Even though there are a few steps to take while you are setting up and managing your own Etsy shop, selling your items on the platform is a pretty simple process overall. So, let's dive into how Etsy can work for you.

THE ADVANTAGES OF ETSY

So, what advantages are there in using an Etsy store to showcase your products? Why not use some other platform? Or better yet, why not make your brand's own website? Well, if you make an Etsy shop then it comes with a lot of useful advantages.

First and foremost, Etsy has a well-known reputation and is already well-known with people who love handicrafts. Finding people to sell to requires you to create a new audience, effectively starting from zero. On the other hand, there are currently millions on Etsy who are eagerly looking for products like yours. That means you start with a customer base that's already interested in the kinds of products you might be thinking of selling.

Even better, with an online platform like Etsy, customers are not confined to your town because you have eliminated the necessity for a physical location. If you were planning to open a physical store spanning many towns, you would have to spend on all kinds of assets, such as storage, equipment, sites, personnel, contractors, and advertising for each sales site. On the other hand, selling your designs on Etsy gets you worldwide exposure for a minimal investment of time and money. That means you can take things at your own pace without having to do everything all at once.

When a shop is first getting started, it needs a lot of advertising. The good news here is that you can count on the fact that on Etsy, you can tap into a large pool of millions of people who will almost certainly be interested in what you have to sell. It's more than enough to just work on your store, and emphasis can be placed on product types and categories. This helps customers who are on the lookout for your kind of shop find it with ease.

While every platform has a distinctive audience, charge structures, listing formats, and sales processes, keep in mind that they all have unique customer bases. Currently, Etsy is well-suited for businesses and artists that focus on crafts and offers an existing built-in consumer base suitable for particular kinds of products and crafts. Although other worldwide marketplaces are mostly aimed at customers who value originality, quality, history, and tradition in the goods, Etsy is distinct in that it is primarily focused on customers who want the behind-the-scenes story behind their purchase to be meaningful. The design and structure of your Etsy shop are meant to highlight these particular advantages rather than serving as a model for other e-commerce sites that have the same features for all product categories and do not allow you to stand out in the marketplace. So, if that sounds like the kind of products that you create, then Etsy is a good fit to help you bring your work to a global audience.

To sum up, working on Etsy means a much lower threshold to enter. And that makes it so much simpler and more straight-forward to take your crafts to the world. By allowing you to quickly and efficiently process your orders without the intricacies and headaches of a traditional business, Etsy makes it simpler for you to work on your crafts.

HOW TO OPEN UP YOUR OWN ETSY SHOP

Now you might be wondering how hard it is to open your own Etsy shop. Here comes the good news. Starting your own shop through Etsy is a simple and straight-forward process. Have a look at the steps and you can decide for yourself if it's right for you.

Step 1: Create an Etsy Account

Setting up an account with Etsy is easy. Just go on the site, click on the "Sell on Etsy" link, enter your personal information, and then click "Register." If you have a Google, Facebook, or Apple account, you can also create your account through them.

Step 2: Set your Shop Preferences

This step is simple and just establishes your preference for language, currency, and home location.

Step 3: Choose the Name of your Shop

We'll talk more about this in Chapter 3, but make sure to give your shop's name a lot of thought.

Step 4: Add Items to Your Shop

Once you've got a shop name, it's time to start listing the items you're selling. Remember that you need to list each one separately and take photos for each. This is also where you'll list the price of what you're selling. Selecting the price for your product can be tricky and we'll go into detail about it in Chapter 5.

Step 5: Choose your Payment Preferences

Pick how you want to accept payment for your product. There are a lot of options including PayPal, check or money order, and Etsy Payments which you can use to accept credit and debit cards.

Step 6: Set up Billing

This is where you establish how you'll pay the different fees that Etsy charges to use its platform. This step will depend entirely on where you're located. In some countries, Etsy will ask for a credit card in order to prove identification. If you're based in the United States, then you can enroll in auto-billing.

Step 7: Open Your Shop

Once you've finished setting up all the back-end things like billing and preference and you've listed some of your items, you're ready to go public! Just click on the button "Open Your Shop" and anyone can see your store.

Step 8: Make your Shop your Own

This step should be an ongoing process as you continue to make your Etsy shop something unique to you. This is the step when you add your photo and bio and establish the feeling of your product. This is also when you should start establishing some policies for shipping and turn-around time.

GET READY FOR THE ADVENTURE

Now you should have some idea of what it takes to set up your own Etsy shop and start selling your crafts to people around the world. Getting started is pretty simple, but there's more to it than that. That's why we'll go over some other fundamentals like how to choose what you'll sell, how to price your crafts, brand-building, and the importance of shipping. So get ready, because the adventure is just beginning!

2. WHAT TO SELL

I f you've decided to open an Etsy shop, the first thing to decide on is - what product will you sell? Remember, everything starts with your product. This is the starting point and the cornerstone for your shop, and it will inform a lot of what you will do next. Maybe you know exactly what you want to sell. Or maybe you're still going over a few different ideas. Or maybe you have no idea.

DON'T START WORRYING!

Take your time to consider what you might want to work on and what crafts you might be interested in making. This is where you can let your personality really shine through and show off your skills. So, before you decide anything, we have a few tips for how to choose what you should sell.

POSSIBLE PRODUCTS YOU CAN SELL

Etsy has a huge list of products for sale to its customer base. But the big question still remains - What are you ready to sell?

Now is the time to think more about what it is that you want to create. If you already know, that's fantastic! If not, don't worry! Consider what you're passionate about and see if that fits. If you still don't have an idea, look at lots of different items and try to consider what it takes to make them as personalized crafts.

You may have come to this book looking for ideas because you enjoy making things but do not know what to make yet. In that instance, the idea is to figure out what is hot and then create a new category around it, build a brand around it, and sell things that are hopefully easy to ship.

If you don't know what you want to sell, there are plenty of ways to figure it out. First, try scrolling through a few Etsy shops and other online retailers and see what catches your eye. It's important to think about what *you* would buy. Remember that you're going to be putting in some time into making your product, so it has to be something you care about. If you can't think of what that is, try going through your own Internet history or see what you've spent money on yourself. This should help give you an idea about what kind of crafts you're interested in.

Perhaps, the question still remains - what should you sell on Etsy? Unfortunately, we can't answer it for you, but hopefully, you can find some inspiration here. Below is a list of some jumping-off points that might help you out in deciding. If any of these pique your interest, look into them. Go a bit further and look into what you need to make them and how long the process takes.

Jewelry

Handmade jewelry is one of the most popular and in-demand products on Etsy today. That means bracelets, necklaces, and earrings. Customers enjoy buying these kinds of things for themselves as well as giving them as gifts. Think of ways that you can make a piece of jewelry unique and give it a personal touch.

Vinyl Mugs

Etsy has a surprising number of vinyl mugs for sale. These mugs frequently feature unique artwork or slogans and are a big hit with the Etsy community. This is one starting point since you mostly need blank mugs and can adjust them according to your own creativity. Moreover, you can outsource the production of your vinyl mugs and then sell them for a profit.

Baby Items and Kids Toys

Customers on Etsy frequently search for baby products such as headbands and silicone teethers. Other baby things, such as personalized boxes to keep goods in, are also very popular. Handmade wooden toys are all the rage these days as well. Look through these and see which (if any) fit best with your creative energy.

Planners and Stickers

You might be shocked at how popular planners and stickers are on Etsy. You could offer calendars and stickers. There will be printing and other expenses to factor in, but the threshold to entry is quite low.

Pet Products

People in the United States, Canada, Europe, and around the world adore their pets, so it is no wonder that pet-related items sell well on Etsy. The best-selling items will be those for dogs and cats. However, you could also find a niche market for less common pets like snakes, lizards, and ferrets. This is another category that has a lot of different options from collars, bowls, toys, anything else that pet-lovers might want. Moreover, by personalizing pet items, you will be able to sell more of them.

Sewing Supplies and Patterns

Sewing supplies including zippers, swatches, fabric, and embroidered patches can be found in some extremely successful Etsy shops. You do not have to make these things yourself, which is always a plus. Sewing patterns are also becoming extremely popular. This is a great choice if you regularly sew and like creating through. If not, it may not be for you.

Self-Care Products

Self-care items are constantly in high demand on Etsy. This includes bath products, essential oils, artisan soaps, massage oils, and lip balms. If you happen to find a wholesale supplier with great quality of products, you could be well on your way to great success. The tricky part is finding a way to personalize these products to make them your own and distinct from others.

Phone Cases

Mobile phone cases are in high demand on Etsy, which should come as no surprise. A lot of people invest in making their state-of-the-art mobile phones look aesthetic. Cases that are both attractive and protective of the phone will always sell well.

Wedding Products

Weddings and anniversaries are special events where people want something totally unique for their special day. This can include a whole range of crafts depending on what you want to make. Common wedding products include handmade invitations, decorations, décor, corsages, and more.

CONSIDERING YOUR PRODUCT

Now that we've gone over a few ideas, it's time to think it over. When you think you might know what you want to sell, consider the following.

Do you enjoy making it?

You can't fake enjoying the process, so it's important to be honest with yourself. You have to choose a product that you actually like creating or your creativity won't shine through. Worse yet, if you don't like making it, then you might come to resent it.

Is it popular?

This question is a bit tricky to answer since trends can change quickly. Another way to think of it is 'will there be an audience that wants your product?' While you don't have the popular things out there on the market, you should have at least a few potential customers. If you're finding that your idea has a small audience, try making it broader. For example, if you're thinking about making collars for ferrets, think about also making collars for other pets.

Does your product offer opportunity to expand?

This is another more challenging question, but it's important to think about. Can you create variation on your product in order to offer something new? If you're making a craft supply, can you alternate the colors? If you plan to sell some kind of clothing, can you alter the pattern or the design? The more ways you can provide variation to customers, the better!

How much work does it take to make your product?

This is one of the most important considerations you'll have to make when choosing which product you plan to sell. We recommend looking over the process of making lots of different products and seeing which is possible. You need to consider a few things like:

- How long the process takes
- How difficult it is
- What materials you need

The amount of time it takes to make a product can vary, but you should pay some specific attention to the materials that are required. It's important to know whether the materials needed to make a craft are available wherever you are. And if they are, you also need to see if they are at a price that's within reason. Looking at materials is an absolutely essential step here. You have to consider this carefully because if the materials needed to make something aren't available or are too difficult to get a hold of, you're going to run into problems.

AN EXAMPLE IN CREATING A PRODUCT

By now you should be considering both the materials for your craft as well as the process to make them. If either one of these doesn't work well for you, then you may need to rethink things. To show you more precisely what this means, let's look at an example. We're going to look over what it takes to create candles. That includes the materials as well as the actual steps making a candle takes. The process itself is only nine relatively simple steps. Likewise creating a batch takes roughly an hour, so it's not a huge time investment either. Additionally, the number of materials that you need is actually quite low. All of these has been simplified a bit, but it should give you an idea of what goes into making a candle.

- Candle Making Supplies
- Wax
- Wicks
- Candle contains (glasses, tins, jars, etc.)
- Melting pot
- Masking tape
- Scale
- Thermometer
- Whatever fragrances you'd like to add

Candle Making Steps (simplified)

1. Measure the wax
2. Melt the wax
3. Add fragrance oils
4. Prepare the candle containers
5. Attach the wick
6. Pour the wax
7. Secure the wick
8. Add more wax
9. Cut the wick

If you're looking at these nine steps and getting ideas, that's great! But also try to remember that this is just the outline of a recipe. In reality each craft, candles included, needs something personal to make it stand out.

While the process above should take about sixty minutes, you're still going to have to do a lot of experimentation to create the end result that you want to provide to customers. For example, at step one you need to measure out the wax and deciding on the right amount will depend on your end-goal. The same is true of step three, where you add the oils. You can go online to get loads of advice on what kind of essential oils to add, in what quantities, and in what combinations. However, at the end of the day, you're going to have to experiment for a while before you find the perfect formula.

DO YOUR RESEARCH

Once you have a specific craft in mind that you want to sell, now's the time to do some more research on it. Find out everything you can about it. Consider the following:

- How is it made?
- Can you make it at home?
- Will you need special tools?
- How long does it take to create?
- What materials do you need to make it?
- Who's buying this product?

As we said before, the product is the cornerstone of your Etsy shop, so you need to be sure of everything before you decide.

Ask yourself a few more questions

Do you have a higher level of craftsmanship than the competition? Is it true that your nearest opponent is a thousand miles away? Are there not enough products out there to cover all the needs? The goal of this exercise is to figure out not just whether or not you will sell, but also who will buy it. This brings us to the following topic.

Who is Your Target Audience?

Make no mistake about it, without a target audience you can't just put your product out there and expect to get immediate results.

To put it as simply as possible, you need to think about the people who will be interested enough in your product to purchase it.

The best method to figure out what you want to achieve is to think about it from your own perspective. What piqued your interest in the product? What prompted you to do this? Who was the first to buy it when you first offered it? Do you think this product is appealing to you? Would you purchase this product if it were made available to you? You can get a basic profile of your potential clientele by answering these questions. Then, based on your observations and the people who are identified as customers of similar products from your competitor, you can learn more and expand your audience further.

It is possible that people do not know about your product if there is very little or no interest in it. If your study shows that there will be a sufficient demand for what you have to offer, you can go ahead and open your shop. It's also always a good idea to check on similar products. Ask yourself if people are selling something similar. Then you should also wonder Is your product unique in a particular way? If you're creating something one-of-a-kind, the answer is straightforward. You have no competition. If you are making handcrafted items that are comparable to or identical to those sold by others, then it is time to think about why customers would choose your products over their competitors.

Look at Trends

Once you've got your idea, you may want to look at trends to see what a good starting point might be. For this, the trend monitor on Etsy is a page for trending products that can be useful. Sites like Twitter, Buzzfeed, and Google all have capabilities that allow you to see what people are searching for. It would be beneficial if you set up notifications for this and keep your eye on some social media. You should watch out for what's hot on Amazon, eBay, and Pinterest, and subscribe to a few craft and design websites and magazines. Don't just go along with what everyone else is doing, but do not wait for anything to go out of trend either. It is frequently beneficial to go from one concept to another. Is anyone making mini letters that you may send to your friends? What other little creations could you come up with?

Something different

Once you have finished doing your research and find a product that appears promising, find a way to make that craft into something truly distinct. On Etsy, one of the main things that draws people in is the knowledge of getting something different, personal, or one-of-a-kind. As such, having the highest quality product is not always important and having one that is truly unique is not always necessary. It is all about giving it a distinctive feeling.

After you have considered how to make your own product unique, you might want to start creating fresh and high-quality products that adhere to a theme or ethos. This is something else that can make your work stick out. Having a sort of creed that you have established can help keep customers engaged and coming back. Think about working with a particular material that people like all of the time, whether it is because it is authentic or because you only use organic materials. You might then try to establish yourself as a thought leader in that sector among bloggers and continue to grow in this manner so that you are aware of new advancements and people will begin to seek out your items after hearing what you have to say.

The difference between leather and Italian leather is minor, but given the option which would you choose? Beef stew can be found all around the British Isles, but in America, it is invariably referred to as Irish stew for no apparent reason other than marketing. On Etsy, you have a limited amount of room to develop your brand, but you can make sure that your product stands out even if it is similar to others. Whether it is the material, pattern, style, or location, try to pick something you haven't seen before and make it your own thing. You'll never beat a big brand in the sneaker industry, but you may be number one in a category that you've created, like vegan hemp sneakers.

Hopefully, this has helped your creative juices flow and think about a few different ideas for what to sell. There really is no wrong answer to this. The main thing is to be sure that the product you choose is something that:

- You can make (materials and process)
- People want
- You want to make

If you've got those three basic tenants covered, then congratulations! If not, give it more time. And once you've settled on the sort of product you want to see, it's time to start setting up your store.

3. SETTING UP YOUR SHOP

Once you've decided on your product, it's time to set up shop. This is one of the most important steps because your Etsy shop is how customers view your product. You need to pay attention here because every detail counts! The way you showcase your product is an important aspect of the customer's overall experience with your store and brand. The customer's first view of a product photo sets the tone for the rest of the presentation, which culminates in the customer's hands-on encounter with the product.

We talked about setting up your shop in Chapter 1, but let's go into a few more details. It's important to list your product with good descriptions and photos so that you can attract people who are interested in what you have to sell. Let's go over some of the important steps here.

- Create your account
- Select a Shop Name

- List your product
- Take photos of your product
- Writing product descriptions
- Use Search Engine Optimization to your advantage
- Selecting a Name for your Etsy Shop

Once you've created your Etsy account, the very first thing you'll have to do is select a business. This can be a daunting task, especially since once you choose your name, you can change it. So, let's talk about what a name on Etsy means.

CHOOSING A NAME

The name of your store or shop is an extremely important thing to think over. First impressions are so important, so having a name that stays with people might make or break your business. Customers may choose to visit or ignore your store when they see its name. With that in mind, you must select a name that will allow you to attract as many clients as possible. Remember that the name is important for style, searchability, and audience recognition. Here are some pointers to help you choose the best name for your store.

Reflect what you are selling as much as possible

You can choose a name that contains the specific things you are selling if you want to make it easier for people to find your business. If you are selling custom coasters, for example, make sure your store name includes the word "coaster." When customers looking for coasters see your store's name, they will be lured to it right away and come in. Moreover, choosing a name like things helps with search engine optimization, so when potential customers look for your product, they're more likely to find yours. On the other hand, there is a disadvantage to doing so. If you decide to broaden your product line, you may have a difficult time finding clients, especially if they have already come to connect your store with coasters.

Pay attention to Spelling

You should try to choose a name that is simple to spell and pronounce. While it is strongly advised that you create an original and distinct name, you should avoid making things difficult for your clients by utilizing odd or uncommon words. You should also be sure before deciding on a name with special characters. Sticking to conventional terminology and accurate spelling should be your goal since potential clients will have an easier time remembering and putting the name of your shop into the search bar if you do it this way. Customers may mistype your store's name and be sent to another shop if you choose a name that is difficult to spell. When this happens, you risk losing consumers. You are well aware that fewer clients are detrimental to your company's success.

Maintain brevity and simplicity

You should try to avoid giving your shop a long name as much as possible. It is not only tough to remember, but it is also time consuming to type. As a result, you should attempt to keep the name of your shop simple and to the point. Using more than three words is not recommended.

Take a test to see how well you remember things

No, you do not need to take this test at a testing center. You can do it on your own time and from the comfort of your own home. It is actually quite straightforward. Take a pen and a piece of paper and attempt to recollect which Etsy stores piqued your interest. Make a list of the names of these stores. It makes no difference whether or not you enjoy the products sold in that store. All you have to do now is write down the names of the stores that come to mind. After you have finished, check over these names and see if there is anything you can find in common with them. Consider what makes them memorable and appealing to the ear. Then, as a starting point for naming your shop, utilize them as inspiration.

Use the search engines to find what you are looking for

Try using whatever search engine you can think of including Google, Bing, Yahoo to search for the product your plan to sell. Then after you have typed in your preferred name, look at the first page of results. Do you believe you have what it takes to be on the first page of Google's search results? It might not be a smart idea to go with a name if the search already pulls up a lot of stores, blogs, or websites with a similar name since it will be harder to distinguish your brand.

Don't use names or terms that are offensive to others

Words that are considered profane or offensive are not permitted on Etsy. As a result, you must use extreme caution while choosing terms. Make sure you pick the proper name on your first try, because starting a new business purely on the basis of its name can be tough and frustrating and it can be tough to bring customers in to your new shop if you have already established a following under your previous name since it will be exhausting for you to move your belongings. Worse still, you won't be able to transfer any of your previous sales records, discussions, feedback, or other interactions to your new shop.

Make Sure the Name You've Decided on Isn't Taken

You definitely do not want to get sued over the name of your Etsy shop. So, before you make a final decision on your shop's name, make sure you follow the regulations in your state and/or country. It is important to keep in mind that some names and words have already been registered as trademarks. As a result, they are no longer permitted to be used. By contacting your Secretary of State, you can find out if a name has already been registered. You can also visit the website of the United States Patent and Trademark Office. In addition, you can seek legal guidance from a professional.

Let your personality and sense of flair shine through

Choose a name for your store that reflects the owner's personality and the merchandise's style. If you are selling entertaining and unusual things, for example, you should create a name that fits them perfectly. Choose a name that is attractive or refined if you are selling traditional items. When coming up with a name for your store, do not be scared to let your imagination go wild. After all, you want people to think of your store when they think of you and your products.

LISTING YOUR PRODUCT

Taking Winning Photographs

Photographs are really important when it comes to selling on Etsy, or anywhere else. Because you do not have a physical store in which your customers can browse your products, you have to provide outstanding visual aids. Photos are not quite as good as the real thing, but they give the viewer a good idea and strong impression. This is why you must do everything in your power to upload the best photographs available. Your prospective buyers should be able to acquire a sense of how your products look and feel by looking at these photographs. Here are some helpful hints for uploading photos to your Etsy store:

Invest in a high-resolution camera

You should use a high-quality camera as much as possible to ensure that your images are of the highest possible quality. You can choose from a wide variety of digital cameras. Before making a final purchase, make sure you read reviews and look through the specifications. You can use your smartphone if you cannot afford a more expensive one. Do not worry; even if you only used your phone, there are strategies you may do to improve your photographs. These methods will be covered in greater detail later in this book.

For close-up images, use the macro settings on your camera

The majority of the things sold on the site are small enough to fit into the macro setting. A flower or tulip icon is commonly used to represent this setting. You do not, however, have to limit yourself to just one setting. Feel free to try out different settings until you find one that suits you the best. Experiment with different combinations to determine what works best.

Avoid using a flash camera

Some merchants make the mistake of photographing using a flash camera. Take note of the images you took with your camera's flash switched on and compare them to the ones you took with the flash turned off. You will notice that images taken without a flash seem significantly better. This is due to the fact that the flash produces a light that bounces off the subject and distorts the image. Go somewhere where the lighting is bright but diffused if you want your images to appear brighter. Because the lighting is bright and natural, it is perfect to snap shots outside.

Use natural lighting instead of artificial lighting

The ideal lighting for capturing photos is outside. Standing in direct sunlight, however, is not recommended. This will degrade the quality of your photographs. Instead, capture the images in a light that is not direct. Place yourself in the shade or somewhere that is not immediately exposed to the sun. You could, for example, stay on the patio.

Use different props to your advantage

Using props in conjunction with your merchandise can result in stunning photographs. You can buy props from specialty stores or make your own using items you already have around the house. Flowers, for example, can be used to make your products appear more charming and classy. Small toys can be used to complement a baby's outfit. You can also decorate the photos with balloons, books, and other appropriate materials. Herbs, for instance, make excellent props for handcrafted soap and shampoo.

A mannequin can also be used to display hats and other items of clothing. If you do not have any props, you can model the item using your own body. On a solid color background, an apron would appear better on you than a plain color background. Wrapping a scarf around your neck would be more attractive than simply lying down on the floor. Wearing samples of your products will allow potential customers to see how they will look in real life. On the other hand, make sure you do not go too far. Keep in mind that the item, not the props, must be the focal point or major focus of the images. Even if you employ appealing props, your items should be the ones that draw attention.

Select a background that will draw attention to your item

Backgrounds are important in photography. You can utilize printed or patterned backgrounds if you do not have any props to go with your things. Make sure, though, that the background is not too distracting. You could alternatively choose a plain background. Any solid color will do, although white and black are the best options. Except for white products, a white background complements almost anything. White, gold, silver, or neon-colored goods, on the other hand, look best against a black background. Keep in mind that contrast is important in this situation. You should select a darker background if your objects are in light or pastel hues. If your objects are dark in color, on the other hand, you should utilize a lighter background.

Take pictures from various perspectives

Make sure to photograph your item from many perspectives so that your customers can see how it looks from the front, back, sides, top, and bottom. Take a few shots from each viewpoint and sort them afterward, selecting the best images from each viewpoint. Etsy allows sellers to upload up to five photos per listing, so be sure you include all of the images you require. A photo should be included that displays how your item appears from various angles. Make sure to include both close-up and full-size photographs in your submission. Customers will be able to see all of the product's details this way.

Use a photo editor to enhance your photographs

When we say edit, we mean that you should improve the appearance of your things rather than completely changing their appearance. In the photos, your item should still appear the same so don't lead your potential clients astray by making your products look to be something else. To boost the quality of your images, upload them to a photo editor after you have taken them. Photo editors come in handy when it comes to making images appear as if they were taken by a professional photographer. Adjusting the contrast and removing the background noise are two examples of what you can do. You can also use a copyright watermark to protect your images. This way, you can be confident that no one else takes your photos and utilizes them for their own gain. However, you can still enable others to use your images, possibly as a source of inspiration, as long as they acknowledge and ask your permission first. More on photo editing will be discussed in the following section.

Give context

When objects stand alone in a photo, it can be hard for potential customers to discern their size. This is why you must convey a sense of scale to your customers. This can be accomplished by photographing your things with yourself or a model. It can also be displayed next to a pet or other familiar object.

If you offer handcrafted dolls, for example, your buyers may not realize how small or large they are unless you show them next to something they already know the size of. So, if you are selling this doll and it is only the size of your palm, you can prop it up on your palm and photograph it. Instead of just laying it down on the ground and snapping a photograph, this would give your buyers a better impression of how big it is. If you are selling an artwork, you can display it on your wall and photograph it. You can either hold up or put on a piece of jewelry if you are selling it. You may also use a mannequin to display it on. The same may be said of apparel. You can either put the clothing on a life-size mannequin or wear them yourself.

Writing Effective Descriptions

A quality product description is essential for captivating customers as well as assisting them in learning more about your goods. As a result, they may be more likely to make a purchase. The right works can persuade potential buyers to add your things to their cart. If you are new to Etsy, you might find that your product descriptions are hard to write. However, with practice, you will be able to write great product descriptions in no time. The following are some general rules of thumb to remember if you want to be a successful seller on the site

Don't bury the lede

The most crucial information about your item should be the first thing visitors notice in your description. This gives potential customers fast access to information about your product. You can optimize the way this description appears in the search results in addition to giving them juicy details through it. Do not worry; you can utilize words that you have already used in the title of your item.

Make things personal

While people always want to communicate with others on a more personal level, you have a limited to space to make a connection with a potential client. Consider using the first person, you may establish a personal connection with your potential customers because this is a highly effective method. So, rather than just being a faceless salesperson, you should exhibit some personality to your customers. Consider your product descriptions like a first encounter with new acquaintances: you want to appear natural while remaining courteous.

Use bullet points and short paragraphs to make your writing easy to read

You should keep in mind that some of the consumers who come into your store are looking for a specific material or size. To make things easy for them, you should use bullet points and short paragraphs to arrange and make crucial data more visible. Avoid employing words that are not required or that do not make sense. You must be direct and clear about what you are attempting to communicate to potential customers. That way, if your product description is not convincing enough to persuade a potential consumer, your links can guide them to other portions or sections of your shop where they can learn more about you and your products. They might be sent to your About Page, where they can read about your personal success story, aspirations, and objectives for your shop. Potential clients may be persuaded to conduct a business transaction with you after learning more about you and your shop and developing a personal connection.

Discover your own unique voice

Keep in mind that the distinctive style or personality of your shop is established by your writing voice. When it comes to crafting your voice, keep your target audience in mind. Consider what you are attempting to communicate to these individuals. What kind of way of life do they lead? Is your target market mostly made up of mothers with young children or teenagers who prefer to accessorize with the latest and most fashionable accessories? If the majority of your customers are ladies looking for gifts for their boyfriends or husbands, or guys who are engaged and about to be married, you can adapt your product listings to meet their needs. Men's apparel, watches, perfume, and other personal goods are among the products that can be sold.

Questions Your Descriptions on Etsy Should be Able to Answer

Aside from the aforementioned pointers, you should be able to provide answers and solutions to the most common customer concerns and problems. Keep in mind that the majority of these one-time buyers will not be able to pick up your items, feel their texture, smell their scent, or try them on. This is why you must provide them with the information they require as if you were their eyes, ears, nose, and skin.

If the descriptions of your items pique potential buyers' interest, they are more likely to click "add to basket" rather than "back" and never return to your store. To put it another way, your product descriptions are critical to a successful sale. To assist you, the following are some of the most often asked consumer questions for which you must be prepared.

What distinguishes and differentiates your products?

Something should be included in your product descriptions, preferably a story. This story should be compelling enough to persuade others to make a purchase and return to your store in the future. However, such a story doesn't have to be long. It should, however, be long enough to develop a place in the life of a potential buyer for your goods. Take soda advertisements, for example. Have you ever seen a popular brand's ingredient-focused advertisement? Probably not since after all, marketing is primarily about selling a sensation or a want. It is vital to establish a relationship with your customers. So, if you only utilize a product description to highlight the physical characteristics of your things, you are missing out on a tremendous opportunity to make an impression and touch potential buyers' hearts.

What distinguishes them from other goods that are similar to them?

Even while Etsy products are handcrafted, customized, and not mass-produced in a factory, there is a chance that yours is not the only one of its sorts on the site. There is a good chance you are not the only one who manufactures and sells similar goods. If you sell knitted apparel, for instance, you should expect other vendors to sell knitted apparel as well. Knitted sweaters and other clothing are rather common, so you will want to make sure yours stands out.

So, how do you stand out with your products? For one, you can show and explain how your items have a competitive advantage. What distinguishes your products from those of your competitors? What are the qualities and characteristics of your product? Make sure to highlight the unique aspects of your products while remaining respectful to other sellers. You might also describe how your items would make your clients' lives easier, more enjoyable, or more convenient.

What is the total number of products included?

For most goods, the amount is self-evident. Others, on the other hand, will need to be explained clearly. You must specify how many pieces your customers will receive once they have paid for your product. This is often the case with craft items and greeting cards. Handmade envelopes and other types of stationery are in the same boat.

Is your purchase the right size for you?

This is especially important for objects that are intended to be worn. Measurements should be included for shirts, blouses, slacks, skirts, and anything else that a person might wear. A model or mannequin can be used to photograph socks, hats, and other accessories. To illustrate the objects on a scale, you must display them on a mannequin or model. Otherwise, determining whether they are too little or too large for the wearer would be difficult. The key goal is to show your buyers how the item will look on them.

What is the purpose of the object?

You must always include one or two 'action shots.' These show your product in its proper context. This is particularly true if your stuff is intended to be used in conjunction with another item. If you are selling an iPad stand, for example, you will need to illustrate your product holding an iPad. If you are selling a cellphone case, you will need to demonstrate it using a phone. You must have a real passport featuring the passport holder if you are selling bespoke passport holders. What if your product is something that can be downloaded? Let us pretend you are a seller of downloaded recipe books. You can demonstrate your recipe to potential consumers by preparing a dish and then displaying the recipe beside it. This will provide your prospective clients a sense of how the finished dish will look and what they can expect when they buy and download your virtual recipe book.

What are the materials that you use in your products?

It is critical to inform your customers about the resources you utilized to create your items. By doing so, you may offer customers an impression of the product's quality and durability. If you are selling furniture, such as tables and chairs, you should specify whether you utilized wood, metal, or a combination of the two materials. If you used wood, you should specify the type. As you may be aware, different varieties of wood have different feelings and varying degrees of strength. Some are more durable than others, and they tend to endure longer. You should also let them know about the finish and other methods you employed to create the item. If you're selling clothing, the components you utilized should be mentioned in the description. Fabric, dyes, stains, zippers, buttons, and other accessories should all be considered. The majority of Etsy customers are also looking for natural products. So, if you are selling modeling clays, face masks, lotions, soaps, and other similar items, make sure to include whether they are organic, hypoallergenic, gluten-free, or low in volatile organic compounds (VOCs) in your product description.

Is your product ready-to-wear, a pattern, or a special order?

Unfortunately, a large number of customers make the error of not specifying this. They are, however, all distinct, which is why you must be specific when discussing them in your descriptions.

Obviously, a finished product is a 'pre-made' or 'already produced;' a 'custom order' is something that a customer desires to be done or something that is unique; and a 'pattern' is a raw product or a guide that consumers need to create the final product themselves. Why is it necessary to specify which of these three it is? Even if the products are not fully ready-made, merchants may display images of them. Instead of publishing a snapshot of the pattern, they might upload a photo of a finished object that incorporates the pattern. Your buyers may believe that they are paying for the same products in your images if you sell custom order items or patterns. To minimize misunderstandings, specify whether the item is ready-made, a pattern, or a bespoke order in your description.

Using Search Engine Optimization to your advantage

Search Engine Optimization (or SEO) is a method of raising the number of visitors to your website while also boosting the quality of your traffic, to enable it to rank better in organic search results. So, how does this affect you? Similar to social network accounts, Shopify, and Amazon profiles, your Etsy store, and any products that are registered in it, will appear in Google searches when someone searches for a certain product or your company's name. In order to get both a good ranking on the platform and the ability to find products similar to yours when people perform searches in search engines, you want your shop to rank well. These search queries are known as organic search queries since they are not influenced by any other sort of web advertising or SEO methods (e.g., Google, Etsy, or social network adverts, or an alternative website's link or banner placement). The more visibility you can gain on Etsy and on search engines, the more SEO methods you will have to employ.

That sounds difficult…Can I Really Do It?

Some people believe SEO optimization contains a multitude of secret hacks, and that the best practices are either done by spending money on advertising or having highly skilled IT specialists write unique codes that are inserted into the website or the written content. But, in reality, it's a lot easier than that.

In reality, search engine optimization boils down to a series of guidelines that you should follow to help search engine algorithms recognize your website or your content as a relevant result for certain search queries.

How exactly does Etsy SEO work?

Since Etsy will already be available on all the major search engines, you don't have to worry about any of that. If you want to work with search engine optimization, then it's rather simple. The main thing to do is look at what specific phrases and wordings have more hits on different search engines. This could be seeing whether 'patent leather' or 'Italian leather' have more hits and changing your store's descriptions based on that.

This is something to consider when thinking about the name of your Etsy store as well. Having a more searchable name can bring in a lot more views to your store, so it's worth considering.

Going Deeper with SEO

To understand search engines, it is important to understand that they are more than forms you fill out while browsing for a website. You are provided with a list of outcomes that has been based on the engine's assessment of the best quality content to show for a certain topic. To know if your question has been answered by the search engines, search engines evaluate which websites provide the best answers. But, how exactly do they go about doing that?

In order to illustrate a more sophisticated process, we chose an allegory that is both simple and true. When you think about it, no library employee is conducting research on search engines, and it is quite certain that no youngster is handling that task. Though popularly referred to as "crawlers," search engines like Google actually use web crawlers to gather the information that they locate online. Information is indexed by crawlers, who subsequently return with the results. That data is then sent through an algorithm that performs matches between reader queries and available information. Search Engine Optimization (SEO) can have a massive impact on your website; however, your experience may vary greatly depending on these considerations:

Traffic/content quality. When you are writing material, these two points are intertwined because you need to be aware of the content's attraction to the target reader. Even if your reader is seeking out an organic facial cream, they will not be satisfied if a hair product store appears in the search results. If you want quality content, focus on being on-topic and giving valuable information.

Quantity. In this case, the number of visitors coming to your website (and hence, the number of individuals) will increase as the amount of traffic you receive increases. If there are a lot of people looking for your material, and if there is a lot of content to seek for, your material will be popular. Depending on your website's ranking, your store may rank high or low.

Organic searches. This organic traffic is the traffic you did not buy to receive from search engines. All of the traffic for your store/website originates from people discovering your store/website on their own and then visiting out of interest. Organic traffic is very essential when considering the search engine ranking of a website as opposed to other sorts of traffic.

Search engines can aid to better understand your content by taking advantage of your optimization. The more search engines know about your material, the better they will be able to suggest content to go with it for readers or searchers. SEO is quite versatile, and there are numerous strategies and techniques for doing it. The primary goal of SEO strategies is to optimize titles and meta descriptions. While this is just a small part of SEO, there is so much more to it. Search engine optimization tactics used on your site will help build brand visibility.

You must have content on your website before you can get your point across. To readability optimization, you must first divide your material into pieces, which results in increased understandability. Search Engine Optimization-friendly copies have brief paragraphs with a clear structure. Keywords are to be used in a natural, relevant way to match the logical framework of the material, but they are not to be used excessively. The so-called "keyword stuffing" is responsible for making your content look artificial and less credible. On the other hand, you want keywords to be where they logically belong, and that is exactly what you get when you do so.

4. UTILIZING THE ETSY PLATFORM

F ill up your "About" section next, telling buyers a little more about yourself, why you founded your shop, and what motivates you. You may also include up to five photos and one video to tell the story of your business. Try offering your customers a behind-the-scenes peek at your workplace or production process!

Because online shopping can be impersonal, this is your chance to showcase that you are a normal person with a legitimate brand! Having an 'about' section may help you rank higher in the search engine results, so do not leave it blank!

FINDING THE RIGHT CONNECTIONS

Etsy's community is what sets it apart from Amazon and eBay's markets. Etsy makes a concerted effort to foster a strong sense of community among merchants, consumers, and Etsy workers. Making and sustaining connections in the Etsy community is critical for a shop owner who wants to be recognized by both consumers and sellers—and you do want to be seen by both, because each has a lot of clout. If the connection is there, they may make curated lists, write reviews, and blog pieces, and even celebrate your brand and mission. Indeed, there are numerous ways to improve your profile in the vibrant Etsy community, and doing so can only help to enhance your brand and increase your sales.

Join Teams on Etsy

As you may already know, an Etsy team is a collection of Etsy sellers who have a common interest. Maybe everyone on the crew is a vintage vase vendor, or maybe they all live in New York. Any teams you join are shown in your Etsy profile, allowing potential purchasers to effortlessly jump between your several stores for a more personalized and complete experience. So as your potential customers browse the site, you and your other team members will see that all of your shops and brands will gain more visibility.

Curating a list of things from a range of stores, making sure to include your own, is another approach to form mutually beneficial ties with your fellow Etsy merchants. Send a link to the vendors whose stores you have highlighted after you have published your list. They will most likely want to promote your list, which will bring traffic to your business as well, because your items will be included in your curated list.

You can also reach out to other business owners by producing an article or a blog post on a group of stores that are linked. This type of uninvited marketing fosters a sense of mutual admiration among Etsy users, portraying you as confident in your own shop and having a broad view of the Etsy community. Send a link to everybody whose shop you have mentioned in an article or blog post once again.

You can also find out which Etsy store owners are in your neighborhood and recommend that you all do something community-building together, like go to the same trade show or flea market. Because you and your Etsy coworkers gain a lived and felt experience of one another, the influence of face-to-face engagement can boost your online community. Consider joining a team, promoting your Etsy colleagues on a curated list or in a blog post, and reaching out to Etsy colleagues in your area as this is the type of team activity that really stimulates mutual support.

Get Comfortable with Community Tastemakers

Etsy Tastemakers, as previously mentioned, are organizations of Etsy aficionados who produce lists of their favorite things on the site. These organizations frequently have some form of institutional affiliation, such as an academic or employment relationship, or a shared affiliation with a journal or a well-known retail outlet. When Tastemakers create a list of Etsy items, they are expressing their affinity for specific products and claiming that these things assist to extend the Tastemakers' own businesses.

As a shop owner, your goal should be to get your store on as many of these curated lists as possible. Making contact with Tastemakers and introducing them to your brand is one approach to do this. Here are five things you can do to get closer to your goal.

Perform Research on Today's Tastemakers

Make a list of Tastemakers you are familiar with and who would be a good fit for your brand. Also, have a look at other Tastemakers' curated lists if you are unfamiliar with their work. Add groups of Tastemakers you do not know to your list of Tastemakers if you think they would be a good fit for your business.

Get In Touch with Both Types of Culinary Artisans

Send an e-mail introducing yourself, providing some background on your business, and include photographs of your product, possibly a quotation from a customer review, as well as your desire to be considered for one of their curated lists.

Offer Yourself to These Tastemaker Communities as a Source of Information

You are initiating an uninvited contact, so present yourself as someone who understands about brands and is informing them of something they are interested in the fact that your brand is a wonderful fit for the lists they have already compiled. Extend your gratitude to the creators of these lists.

Suggest A Couple of Items That They May Want to Include in Addition to Your Own

Offer to promote their curated lists on your Etsy website, in articles, or in blog posts if tastemakers are interested in developing their curated lists and impressing followers. Every business aspires to be more well-known and attract more web visitors.

Send a sample of your product to tastemakers to make a real impression

Make an effort to reach out and create ties with tastemakers, as they influence a buyer's judgments about where to shop and what to buy.

TIME

This is where things get a little complicated. How long does it take you to make the product you are selling? According to the data, the most successful Etsy stores are those that are maintained and updated on a regular basis, implying that someone is devoting time to it. If you need to spend the most of your time in your workshop, you might want to consider bringing in a partner, either to assist you make the things faster or to run the store for you, especially if your understanding of the Internet is more limited. It's common knowledge that some artists are only interested in their work.

Within the time constraints, you'll need to factor in the time it will take you to acclimate to Etsy's nuances (there are always secrets in any trade), as well as the time it will take you to set up your shop and make it distinct and easily available to buyers. Do not make a hasty decision here. Uploading your products with a complete description and images can take a long time, especially if you do not already have any or need to take new ones.

PERSONALITY

Etsy is frequently confused with Amazon and eBay, but Etsy has its own personality and attitude. Many things that were quite popular when traded outside of an eBay context did not do as well on Etsy because the shop owners did not understand the need for a different or distinct aesthetic. When doing your research, look through different Etsy shops to gain a sense of the style involved and to get a feel for the site would be quite beneficial.

Aside from all of the above, there is one factor that is critical in every business venture and in all you do in life. Patience is required. Expect it to take at least three months to sell even a single item. This could last six months or even a year for some products. As a result, in order for your venture to succeed, you will need to be persistent.

5. THE COST OF DOING BUSINESS

While the concept of running an Etsy shop is simple, this does not imply that opening one will instantaneously result in a full bank account. There are a lot of things to consider before opening a shop if you want to make an impression on the clientele you want to attract, just as there are with anything else in business and the markets.

One of the most important things to consider is the price of your product. Because you are the one who creates, markets, and sells it, you are the one who sets the price. So, before you choose a price for your goods and publish it in your Etsy shop, there is a lot to consider. When you are figuring out the pricing for your goods, you should include any alterations and personalization, and gift wrapping, this is relevant. When completing a sale from the United States or Canada, sellers are not charged fees for tax transactions (Goods, Services, and Harmonized Sales Tax), but other countries' sellers should incorporate those charges into the transaction fee.

RAW MATERIALS

Because you are selling a physical product, you will have a cost price, which is the amount of money you paid to create it. Some costs are straightforward to determine, such as the amount of fabric required to complete a project, how much rope, or other raw materials. How much money does it add to the final cost if you buy threads by the dozen but only need one to accomplish a project?

It is critical that you take your materials into account. Make sure you have covered all your material costs. It's easy to overlook some of the smaller things, but always keep in mind that every detail matters! Always attempt to be fair in these situations by counting the partial costs of partially used products, such as thread, lace, or buttons.

TIME AND LABOR

Even if you are manufacturing something at home in your spare time, or out of pure passion for the project, you have to charge for the cost of your labor. If you are giving the product the same amount of time as you would a job, you need to be reimbursed. Calculate your own hourly wage based on the amount of time it takes you to complete each component. Alternatively, you can just set a monetary value to your labor cost per piece. This should give you an idea about how much time its costs you and how much that time is worth.

You should assess yourself and your work in comparison to others in your field. You will be able to get a good idea of how much you should be paying yourself this way. If you are in the clothing company, for example, you should do some research to see how much dressmakers and tailors in your area charge. Because you will almost certainly be designing the garments as well, you will need to learn how much clothing designers earn. You could also work as an accountant, administrative assistant, marketing department, or janitor. If you believe you deserve it, do not be afraid to pay yourself more.

OTHER EXPENSES

What are the other costs associated with producing your items? You may have had to purchase an e-book or sit through hours of tutorials to help understand how to produce your goods. To run your business, you may have needed to rent a studio and drive or commute there every day. All of these elements are necessary for the survival and growth of your firm. As a result, you have to take all this into account. But how are you going to put them all into a single price?

It's absolutely essential that you keep track of your spending for anything that has to do with your business. The full list of expenses should contain everything that is involved in making your merchandise. After that, figure out how much you plan to sell each month and divide that amount by your total expenditure.

If you want a more precise price, you should use an accounting tool to keep track of your spending. A software package can be purchased, or a free version can be downloaded from the internet. Also, make sure you have a good understanding of your large investments. If you buy a sewing machine, for example, you must determine how many outfits you can stitch with it. If you ordered a postage printer, find out how long it will survive before it needs to be replaced.

FEES FROM ETSY

You will not be charged to create an Etsy account or set up your shop on Etsy. However, you will be charged fees for sales and product listings, so you may want to expand your selection. When you sell a product, you will be charged a 5% transaction fee. In return, you will just pay $0.20 every individual listing. So, whatever price you are thinking of for your goods, keep these numbers in mind. The following fees will be levied for your transaction:

Processing fees for Etsy payments, which are dependent on your bank.

Listing fees (when you place ads or promote listings on Etsy), including Etsy listing costs that are dependent on your daily budget and competitive listings.

Lack of Insurance, Expensive Tracking, and No Insurance Shipping rates that vary based on carrier and add-ons, such as insurance and tracking.

Payments for currency conversions, which are only required if you offer services or products in a different currency than the one in your account.

Processing fees from PayPal or Direct Deposit. PayPal charges a fixed fee of $0.30 per transaction and 2.7 percent of total revenue from monthly sales.

Additionally, aside from the initial listing price, Etsy will renew your listing after four months and charge a regular listing price for the renewal. If you don't cancel your listing, then it will be automatically renewed unless you have selected to not renew it.

When you have signed up for Etsy's service, you will receive a monthly statement detailing all fees and deductions applied to your account. You should keep in mind that money must be allocated to meet the fees (i.e., if you are personally liable for the fees, then provide sufficient funds), otherwise you will be financially responsible for settling the fees within 15 days. When pricing your goods, you must take into consideration all of the fees and prices, and so you are unlikely to encounter any fees or charges.

Shipping Fees

You have the products and must send them to your clients; as a result, you are also responsible for the shipping costs. So, make sure to include an exact shipping cost so that you do not lose revenue. Since shipping is particularly complex, this guide includes a more fleshed out section on the subject.

TURNING A PROFIT

The final piece you should be considering is profit. After you have included everything else, such as the cost, labor, fees, and shipping, you still have to consider earning money. If you don't take this into consideration, then your new business isn't going to last long. Your profit can be the surplus you are making or the investment you are planning to make to help your company develop. This quantity can start out small and gradually expand as your work grows in popularity.

Etsy is a platform that allows anyone to open their own shop and start making money from it. No money needs to be spent on site designers, no advertising capital is required, no salaries for expert marketers and SEO specialists are required, and no funds are required to purchase the first stock. That is a substantial sum of money to save. However, in order to earn money, you must provide the products, follow the rules, and adhere to a few easy recommendations.

Investing your Profits

When you make a profit, you should think about where you want your company to go in the long run. If you want to quit your day job or pay off your student loans, you will need to figure out how much money you will make. However, it is possible that this will vary depending on what you are marketing and selling. As a result, take into account all of the relevant aspects.

We have learned about customer service, shipping, listing, and fees, among other things. Let us take a look at how you may make actual money on Etsy now.

Consider thinking beyond the box. The majority of individuals believe that if they charge a high price for a product, it will not sell. That is not the case, though. It is critical to consider a product's true worth. Consider the cost of the resources required to build the product, as well as the time and energy it took to make it. Calculate the hourly wage and add some margin to arrive at the ultimate pricing. This is in addition to the fees incurred when selling on the Etsy website (the $0.20 listing fee and 3.5 percent of the sale). Include the shipping cost as well as extra expenses such as shopping labels.

THE COMPETITION'S PRICES

It is safe to suppose that you are not the only one selling baby clothes on Etsy. You are well aware that there are others. Conduct market research on your competition before deciding on a pricing for your product. Is it true that all of their products cost between $8 and $12 each? Then that should probably be your pricing range as well.

Do you believe the clothing you can give will be of higher quality than theirs? Then you could certainly increase your price to $15 per item. However, if you price each of your products at $150, while your competitors' prices are about ten dollars, you are unlikely to sell anything.

6. WORKING ON YOUR BRAND

If you want your Etsy store to be successful, there's a lot to consider. Yes, you have to provide high-quality goods as well as outstanding customer service. All of this, though, is for nothing if no one knows who you are or what your business is about. This is where branding really comes into play.

Brands tell customers a story and give your products a real identity. Moreover, creating and fostering a brand can help your product be even more personal and with handicraft products, having the personal touch can convince potential customers that your product is worth their attention and money.

Consider going to a thrift store or a less well-known and less expensive boutique. Take a look at the price of a basic shirt or blouse. Then, if you want to spend more money, go to a more costly store that sells the same thing. Take a look at the price tag. You will be astonished at how comparable the things are but how different the pricing are. Marketing is mostly to blame for this. The more costly brand receives far more publicity. It could be promoted by a well-known model or celebrity. It could also be seen on billboards and advertisements throughout the country.

All of these marketing techniques are expensive, which is why the more premium brand is so pricey. Also, because it gets more exposure, it appeals to a wider audience. People have a tendency to believe that what they see on television and on billboards as something positive. As a result, people consider the things provided by that brand to be superior to those sold by a lesser-known brand, despite the fact that they are identical. They have the same appearance, feel, and could even be constructed of the same material.

You must develop your branding if you want your company to be successful and gain a large audience. This is how you make your presence known to the general population and stay in people's minds. Everyone should be aware of your store and the things you sell.

Remember that first impressions matter, which is why you should make a good one. Get the attention of potential clients and persuade them to stay with you. Your brand encompasses more than just the products you offer. Your brand is the promise that comes with the shopping experience.

When customers realize they can count on you for a consistent look and feel across all of your products, as well as your banner, product descriptions, photographs, information in your profile, social media presence, and even comments you leave on other sellers' Etsy shops, you have done everything you can to earn their loyalty to your business.

CREATING A BRAND FOR YOUR PRODUCT

Be unique in your approach. You can always look to others for inspiration, but you should never replicate what they have done. Keep in mind that building a successful business relies heavily on creativity. You must sell one-of-a-kind and original things if you want to be a successful vendor. Similarly, you must come up with a distinct and creative name for your shop. You want to create a brand that conjures up vivid images through the use of actual objects. By developing a stronger memory, they can aid in the growth and popularity of your business.

Make it stand out. As a general rule, there are two fundamental needs for any effective internet installment: authenticity and creativity. Aside from committing plagiarism, you will also be fined for simply re publishing content that already exists (plagiarism). In order to do this, you will need to make your book (shop) stand out among the sea of other books. That is a very sensible approach to go about things. First, you would design your brand's identity, and then all of your internet channels that represent it should be aligned to that identity. When it comes to incorporating brand identity and values into design, content, titles, logos, and all other relevant aspects, it means including these things in the design, content, titles, logos, and all other relevant aspects.

You can also utilize words or phrases that have a personal value for you and are likely to excite the curiosity of potential customers. Below is a list of ideas to help you create your own unique brand.

Once you've done all this, it's time to consider how your tale relates to the image you want to convey to the public. Keep in mind that Etsy is primarily concerned with the personal aspect of the shops and their genuineness. Your personal story can have a great impression on your potential consumers and have a substantial impact on your sales prospects. This is why you must select a tale that will make your potential clients feel special and that purchasing your products would increase the value of their possessions. Similarly, your tale should be inspiring so that they feel good about purchasing your products and giving them as gifts. To put it another way, you must determine what your unique selling proposition is, as well as what your product offers to the table in a distinct and consistent manner. Essentially, your unique selling proposition is a way of expressing your items, their value, and the potential expectations of customers. Examine your products carefully and consider what makes them remarkable and distinct. Consider how your handmade mittens distinguish from the other handmade mittens sold on Etsy if you are selling them. Perhaps you are working with a unique yarn or creating custom designs. Whatever your motivation is, you must be aware of it and accept it. As a seller, you should consider the viewpoint of your customers. You will be able to figure out how to provide them what they want and need this way.

There are many different words that can be used to describe the products you are selling. You must determine which are the most appropriate for your product. If you provide dog photography services, for example, you should use roughly twenty words to describe your business. Reduce the number of options on the list until it is down to ten. Continue to whittle down your list of descriptions until you are left with just four. The purpose of this exercise is to assist you come up with adjectives that will help you stand out from your competition. If your competitors are fashionable, stylish, and sophisticated, as well as experienced, you might characterize yourself as soulful, playful, spiritual, and approachable.

While every seller's dream is to have every customer, this is just not feasible. You cannot please everyone and trying to meet all of their requests would be quite tough. You must select a specific demographic or target audience. You should try your best to develop your brand around what appeals to your target clients once you have identified who they are. Find out what they are like by doing some study. What are their ages, where do they live, and what are their hobbies? Try to imagine yourself in their shoes and think as they do.

Once you've worked out your message and the story you want to tell, go back. Consider a few of the following to make your brand feel holistic.

Work to be consistent. Ensure that your brand messaging is consistent across all platforms. For example, if your shop is all about elegance and the things you sell are lovely, make sure your emails, business cards, social media profiles, posters, and flyers are as well.

Make an effort to communicate regularly using these methods. Every piece of packaging should, to the extent possible, communicate your brand. This includes your shop's logo and name, as well as the theme, colors, and font styles you use. Your brand's essential characteristics should be reflected in everything you do.

As you communicate, strive to make everything is crystal clear. To distinguish out from your competitors and be identified by more customers, you must be straightforward. Attempting to please everyone is futile. You will never be able to satisfy all of your customers. You should only target a single demographic but make it a big one.

Find out how you can situate your brand in a competitive landscape, you must first understand who your competitors are.

Find out what your competition are all about by conducting research on them. Keep in mind that positioning is not something you do to your products, but rather something you do to your buyers' brains. It is all about molding your potential customers' perceptions when it comes to positioning. Consider what other people have to say about the things you are offering. Which of these goods do you believe they already own? What new difficulties do you think you will be able to solve? In what innovative ways do you believe you can assist them in making their lives easier and more enjoyable? How do you think you will be able to fill a need by satisfying the demands of clients that other merchants cannot? Similarly, how do you think you will be able to resolve their concerns that other sellers cannot?

Remember that relationships are important in business, just as they are in life. You must cultivate relationships in addition to your business if you want to grow your brand. You should have a good understanding of your consumers' wants, needs, and preferences. As a result, you must figure out how to make these things happen. Remember that the finest marketing technique is social media marketing, which is done for you by other people. Encourage customers to provide comments on your About Page. Using a range of social media platforms to reach out to more people is also a good idea.

Strive to grab the audience's attention. Direct, brave, startling, helpful, real, and memorable are all qualities you must possess.

People will quickly forget about you if you do not do something. It is self-evident that being forgotten is detrimental to any company. You must be known if you want to make money and establish a brand. Customers' attention and recognition are difficult to come by, especially when there are so many different stores to choose from. This is why you must devise methods that will enable you to maintain your competitive edge.

STORE BIO

One thing you can use to grab people's attention is having an engaging and personal store bio. Here is a part where you may fill in the basic information about your brand. To put it simply, sellers that are more successful focus on telling the stories of why they started an Etsy shop, and areas in which they are enthusiastic. This allows a personal and emotional tone to be established with the customers, along with an emotional appeal that will keep them interested. Collectively, this leads to a store being memorable.

STORE BRAND

A popular e-commerce site similar to Etsy that serves a similar demographic requires its customers to create a good impression before they can sell. In short, brand positioning is making your shop a unique entity, and also knowing how to make it stand out from the others. It establishes your store identity, beliefs, and features that customers will see as something they can relate to.

As a rule, constructing a brand requires developing an inspiring story about your firm. A consumer's impression of your products and services is affected by your products and services, as well as their values. When you align your brand with your product lines, branding strengthens the connection between the items and your customers' relationships with each other. The advantage of having brand awareness is that customers enter the store and see if you have new products, visit your social media pages, and wait till you have stocked your products instead of purchasing from another brand. In order to accomplish this, you must make an effective effort to project a distinctive image of your company. While branding is still only beginning with your store, it is nonetheless a vital feature.

People should be able to predict what to expect from you based on your brand. It should let people know what you are passionate about, who you are, and why they should care about your products. You must explain to them the benefits of doing business with you. Keep in mind that having a great brand allows you to acquire new clients while also encouraging existing consumers to stay loyal.

It is all too easy to get caught up in deciding on a name and a theme for your shop. You could only remember it for the colors, typefaces, and photographs on it. However, keep in mind that these features are derived from the spirit of your brand. Before you start worrying about which photos to upload and which themes to employ, you need to understand what this essence is. The following questions can be used as a starting point for determining your brand's essence

WAYS TO CREATE YOUR BRAND

Write A Mission Statement

It should communicate what your brand stands for, what your firm is all about, and what you want to be remembered for at the end of the day. Begin with the big picture of who you are as a company and work your way down from there.

Discuss How All of Your Products Collaborate to Support Your Brand

Is there anything on your shop's page that is no longer in production? Is there anything that has to go because it contradicts or is irrelevant to your mission statement? Should you increase your product line to provide more variations of a popular item for your customers? Consider each item in your store very carefully.

Look At Your Images in A Non-Sentimental Manner

You simply could not afford to be affiliated with something that is not beneficial to your brand. Examine all of the images on your shop's page, including your profile picture, product shots, and logo. Is there anything that stands out in an unfavorable way? If this is the case, remove it and replace it right away.

Look At Your Copy with A Cold Eye

Of course, your copy refers to all of the material related to your store. Is your copy delivering the message you want it to? Is it able to capture the soul of your brand? Is there anything in your writing that detracts from your brand's message? Is there anything that does not seem to belong here? If your brand is all about urban funk and style, but your copy is all about formality, then your copy is incompatible with your brand. If your photographs are exquisite and you want your business to convey a top-tier Tiffany experience, laid-back writing will offer the wrong image. Mistrust is created by inconsistencies like this. It informs discriminating customers who know exactly what they want that your store is not the place to find it. After all, if you do not take the time to make your text work with your photos, why should a potential consumer assume you are just as sloppy with quality control?

Etsy Engagement Strategy Analyzation and Streamlining

What Etsy groups have you been a part of? What are your favorite stores and items, as indicated in your profile? Do these publicly visible decisions reflect your brand in addition to your personal preferences? For example, you may adore argyle socks and artisanal vinegar, but they have nothing to do with the handmade meditation benches in your shop, so do not include them in your Etsy favorites.

Think about Consistency

If one component of your shop takes off unexpectedly, do not let paying customers' passion get in the way of their enthusiasm— even if their favorite product from your shop is not your favorite. If you began out as a shoe company but now sell more belts and accessories, listen to what your consumers are saying as long as it is functioning, which means what your customers like is consistent with your brand. Allowing your preconceptions about your brand to become the adversary of your shop's success is never a good idea.

Finally, once you've decided on the brand identity for your Etsy shop, consider how to convey it visually. This is where you need to think about logos and banners that reflect the story you're trying to tell.

Logo

The shop owner profile will include your personal photo, and the avatar is where you will add your company logo. To help brand recognition, your store logo must coincide with your brand and meet all the criteria for brand identity. To communicate the proper message to the buyers, your messaging must show how your brand values align with the customers' needs. Your brand will be perceived as different depending on the images and fonts you choose, and these two characteristics help to differentiate between luxury and casual, as well as high-end and lower-end brands. As well, the logo should illustrate the attributes and characteristics of your items. In order to choose the parameters for your store logo, simply state what you sell and describe your merchandise in two or three sentences. Take note that the avatar area on Etsy is square-shaped, and if you do any horizontal logos, they will not look good on the website.

Cover photo/Shop Banner

The shop banner helps your store stay memorable, and it establishes the atmosphere, style, and tone of your business. It is a visual depiction of your brand principles and brand identity. If you choose, you can utilize either a large cover photo or a smaller banner advertisement. In my opinion, I strongly advocate utilizing a cover photo since it is accessible both from computers and phones, whereas the banner is only shown to buyers who visit your store from their computers.

7. SHIPPING IS ESSENTIAL

S hipping is one of the most overlooked aspects in maintaining a successful Etsy shop. It's just as crucial to properly package your product as it is to ship it out, so being an Etsy store manager necessitates the ability to ship. The package that your product comes in is also part of your customers' experience. Their reaction to the outward packing provided by the third-party carrier (such as UPS or the US Postal Service) as well as the internal packaging you offer are part of that experience. Everything should be clean, secure, and professional, both inside and out.

Your company card, a cute sticker instead of tape to secure the package, and embellishments like tissue paper and ribbons could all be included in the inner presentation. Packaging is essentially a second opportunity to provide value to your customer and to market your business to them. You encourage the buyer to develop a good relationship with your brand and organization when you elevate your packaging from ordinary to spectacular.

Making your packaging distinct is also one way to promote your brand. When I sell a coffee mug, for example, I will include a K-Cup (coffee shot) wrapped in bubble wrap inside the mug, as well as a message emphasizing to the buyer that it is our mission to go "above and beyond" their expectations. There are a lot of options for to do something like this:

Creating unique mailing labels for your box or envelope
Including a photograph of the item so that when it is delivered, the customer identifies the box/envelope as being your excellent product.

Including a personal message or a little something extra inside the package.

MAKE A SHIPPING PLAN

While developing a sound shipping policy is and should be a top concern, a strategy will only function if you notify your customers about all of the advantages of your delivery plan. If you sell vintage products, for example, you may explicitly explain the need and benefits of shipping insurance to your buyers. Buyers will perceive you as a responsive seller who is always willing to answer questions and assist them through the purchase and shipping process if you communicate effectively.

On Etsy, you should utilize two sorts of communication: forward-facing communication or information, which is material you include on your listings and policies pages, and follow-up communication, which can occur at any point during the purchasing process.

Shop announcements, shipping policies, and item descriptions are all examples of forward-facing messaging. Messages to purchasers, marking things as sent, advising buyers of shipment status, and communicating with your audience are all examples of follow-up communications.

Use your research to build a clear shipping plan once you have completed carrier research and are aware of all your shipping possibilities. Consider the many possibilities that may emerge as you ship things as you design the best possible shipping strategy. The way you wrap an item can help make sure that it doesn't get damaged during transport. Your consumer will be extremely upset if the item is destroyed during the shipping procedure. They may even request a refund, which is clearly not a good thing. Make sure to pack the item using the appropriate packing material.

For most Etsy merchants, figuring out how to ship and handle their items can be a difficult task. Shipping and handling can be time consuming and intimidating because there is so much to consider like shipping labels and seller/buyer protection. Unfortunately, handling and shipping for Etsy, like everything else we have seen so far regarding Etsy, is complicated.

It is impossible to overstate the importance of establishing a reliable shipping plan for yourself. While there is no "follow-this-to-the-letter" shipping and guiding guidebook for Etsy sellers, you can utilize some guidelines below to get your shipping and handling correct and feel comfortable.

FIRST AND FOREMOST, DO YOUR RESEARCH FOR WAYS TO SHIP

The cost of shipping is going to come up every time you make a sale and give your product to a customer. That means that you need to look up the best shipping plan for you. It's critical that you investigate different mail providers' packing alternatives. Keep in mind that the delivery costs for different packages will vary depending on the carrier. When it comes to designing an Etsy shipping and handling plan, the first step should be to study the best delivery options for your items in particular. Keep an eye out for carriers who provide low-cost delivery options and will upgrade shipping if a buyer demands it.

With that in mind, it's not always a smart idea to go with the cheapest shipping option when looking for a shipping partner for your craft business. It is also useful to know what services different shipping companies include in their shipping packages. Signature confirmation, tracking, insurance, and the like are all things to keep an eye out for in this regard.

You will also want to include your shipping estimates as part of your listings once you have calculated your overall shipping cost. You must accurately measure the weight of the package to calculate the total shipping cost. You can accomplish this with a regular kitchen scale and keep track of the weight and measures for future use.

Go to the Etsy community and absorb up all the knowledge you can. Free information about shipping and handling for Etsy sellers can easily be found in the Etsy forums. If you have any questions about shipping, the Etsy community has a thriving network of successful sellers that are ready to offer good advice.

Additionally, make your shop's shipping policy clear to your customers. By openly informing buyers about your overall shipping policies, you're showing them how much you respect their business and protecting yourself in the event of any problems during the purchasing and sending process.

By putting your policies into practice, you can create a shipping routine. Pay close attention to any shipping issues that do not feel quite right and, if necessary, re-evaluate them. Revisit and change your policies when you discover situations where they do not fit the needs of your store. Keep in mind that the only way to develop an effective shipping strategy is to jump right in and learn on the job by conquering shipping challenges.

Here are a few basic packing strategies for each item to help you become more aware of them.

PHOTOGRAPHS, PRINTS, AND PAPER

Use a large envelope and line both sides with cardboard paper. Sandwich the paper, print, or photo between two pieces of cardboard that are somewhat larger than the paper. It should be placed in a huge envelope with the words "DO NOT BEND" printed in red on it.

GLASS ITEMS

Wrap the item with bubble wrap and store it in a box. Make sure the object is completely enclosed in the bubble wrap. To reduce the item's range of movement, the bubble wrap should be tightly packed inside a box. Boldly write the word 'fragile' on the box before shipping it.

JEWELRY

To reduce potential damage to a minimum, lay foam sheets on both the backside and front side of the jewelry. Jewelry can also be shipped in little jewelry boxes packed within a large envelope.

The type, size, and delicate quality of the jewelry will all influence this decision.

BE PATIENT AND DETERMINED

Be grateful for what you have accomplished and congratulate yourself on a job well done after designing a shipping plan, establishing communication channels, and stating your shipping policies. Keep in mind that, no matter how well you prepare for shipping accidents, you will never be able to anticipate every possible scenario.

You may, however, take safeguards by identifying potential issue areas and developing contingency plans for these scenarios. If you intend to ship internationally, for example, be aware of, accept, and allow for longer shipping periods and delays. Knowing this, you may advise and prepare the buyer, reducing the risk of unpleasant surprises on the buyer's end.

It is also crucial that you remain vigilant and prepared for any scenario. When something unexpected occurs, it is advantageous to be told as soon as possible. It is also critical that you develop solid record-keeping skills. Possess proof of delivery. Label your receipts, keep your insurance information, and track your progress in a secure location. If an issue arises, this will assist you in getting to the bottom of it. Keeping records will safeguard you from being held responsible if something goes wrong.

8. MARKETING YOUR STORE

I n order to achieve what you want, you may want to develop solid and thought-out marketing strategy. For the purposes of social media marketing, here are the procedures to take for an Etsy store.

Come up with a strategy: Decide and affirm who your audience is.

Manage your time: Decide how much time you're willing and able to give to your marketing strategy.

Know your market: Knowing your niche market allows you to gain a better understanding of the people who buy your items, as well as their lives and spending habits. Do your research and learn as much as you can about your future customers.

Find your audience: Decide which platforms you'll be using to find your audience and advertise to them.

Select Your Social Media Channels: Identify the platforms where you want to engage with your clients. You can start with the networking sites you're already comfortable with and expand your social media presence as your business and success grow.

Create a content plan: Once you've chosen a social media platform, you'll need to produce content. This can include lifestyle and shopping recommendations, how-to articles, discounts and giveaways, customer testimonials, product updates, and other content ideas are all possibilities for postings. The content you create should be based on the research you've done on your customers.

Track your results: Keep track of your marketing and see what works and what doesn't.

Adjust your strategy: As you keep marketing your product, you'll learn what works and what doesn't, so don't be afraid to change your strategy accordingly.

MARKETING WITH SOCIAL MEDIA

You may use social networking to grow your Etsy shop's loyal customer base. People who use all forms of social media to promote their Etsy businesses usually see a rise in sales. The ideal way to use social media is to notify people about new listings and to provide regular updates to anyone following your store. It is essential to take advantage of the available social media platforms that fit your brand in order to best garner your customer base.

Facebook

For many business owners, a Facebook page is their primary social media platform. It's a good place to start building up solid following on Facebook. Likewise, an Etsy business owner can use the relationships made on Facebook to drive more focused traffic to their shop.

The process of making the page is relatively straightforward. Just remember that Etsy marketing should be done through a business page rather than a personal one. To effectively advertise your Etsy store, you should keep to your brand concept and have that reflected in everything from the text you write to the product photographs. In the 'about' section of the business page, include a link to your Etsy shop so users will be able to access your shop with ease.

Many Etsy store owners have found that Facebook has provided them with a method to connect with their consumers on a more personal level, allowing them to cultivate a devoted customer base. Store owners will be pushed to work more and produce better things as a result of the Facebook fans who become cheerleaders for them.

Other social media sites like Twitter, LinkedIn, Pinterest, Tumblr, YouTube, and Vimeo, can also be used to advertise things listed on an Etsy store. Which one of these that you use should depend on the customers you want to reach.

Email Marketing

For an Etsy shop, email marketing has a lot of advantages. Entrepreneurs should think about using email to assist them expand their businesses and sales. Email is simply a low-cost method of reaching out to your customers. Unlike social media, where you can't be sure whether your postings are reaching all of your fans and potential customers, an email ensures that any marketing content sent to the mailing list lands in the inbox of everyone on the list.

Building a mailing list is the very first step in Etsy email marketing. You can include a sign-up option on your blog or website to encourage visitors to subscribe to your mailing list. To encourage individuals to share their email addresses, offer them special deals and freebies that they can only get after signing up. provide guarantees that their email addresses are safe and that being on the list has some value. The first time you should ask for permission is when you are about to close a deal with a new customer. Ask whether they'd like to get your newsletter, as well as updates on new goods and special discounts. By subscribing to the newsletter, you are giving your permission to send you emails. The second responsibility is to keep that permission by providing appealing and informative information, and readers have the option to revoke permission by unsubscribing at any point when they open the email.

Individuals who have completed an online purchase are more inclined to make additional purchases in the future. The ultimate responsibility is on the Etsy entrepreneur to capture and hold the attention of someone who has expressed a specific interest in a listed goods. You have a better chance of making further transactions with a customer if you hold their attention.

It is not uncommon for a buyer to purchase an item from a firm that provides high-quality goods and then never return for more. It is more likely that the customer just forgot about you, rather than having a negative experience with you or your goods stopping them from returning. Emailing these clients allows you to stay in touch while also reminding them about your Etsy business and offerings.

It is essential to also have a relationship with the customer that goes beyond a string of on-site communications at the moment of purchase. Send out regular emails with useful and entertaining material to remind them of your product line and demonstrate that you care enough about them to educate them. Keep in mind that if you do not contact a one-time customer, you risk losing their business.

You can give your customers your story or the story behind your items every time they make a purchase, for example. It is achievable with the help of email autoresponders, which send out an email to consumers thanking them for their purchase and telling them a little about yourself or your Etsy products. You are indirectly marketing your products by highlighting more information in this manner.

USE EMAIL NEWSLETTERS, FREEBIES, AND COUPONS

It is a great approach to reach out to both existing customers and those who have not made a purchase yet. You may enhance sales, develop your mailing list, and gain loyal consumers by sending out emails with discounted rates, freebies, delivery coupons, and other special offers that are only available to your subscribers.

Use email newsletters to highlight other sellers

It may not seem obvious at first but highlighting another Etsy seller will help you grow your list of subscribers and potential buyers. However, it is recommended that you avoid featuring a competitor because your entire consumer base may leave. Feature Etsy shop owners who have their own newsletter and sell things that are not really similar to yours. You obtain access to the new relevant audience and customers.

Emailing your consumers does not have to be a time-consuming or costly task, especially if you use the correct tools. These tools not only help you develop long-term, profitable connections with your customers and subscribers, but they also help you increase your Etsy shop sales.

There are a variety of online email marketing options that can assist Etsy firms in establishing touch with customers and selling their products. MailChimp, Aweber, and Bravenet are three email marketing providers that provide excellent mailing list alternatives. A little research will assist you in determining the finest service for your Etsy shop.

A regular email newsletter, or even a basic e-mail, can help you expand your business, gain more consumers, and earn more money. Beware though, and tone down your excitement a little because you might overindulge and send way too many emails to your clients, and no one wants that. Your mails might just end up in the spam folder. Send out a monthly email, timed to correspond with new products and special deals.

OTHER FORMS OF MARKETING

Among the most beneficial methods of promoting your product is to create content around them. The content/material that has been developed can be used in a variety of ways to attract new clients. Blogging, website content, and article marketing are all effective opportunities to advertise and sell products.

Blogging

Blogging can be really beneficial for your Etsy shop and products. The key to success, however, is not the blog itself, but the material that goes into the blog. Blogging is far more than a means to boost your products. It is a great way to provide your readers and buyers additional information about yourself, your Etsy shop, and your products. Your blog becomes a place where you may connect with your subscribers and consumers. Blogging may be a very pleasurable activity.

People may pick several platforms for creating and managing their blogs for the purposes of blogging. WordPress is the greatest blogging platform because it is quick, simple to customize, extensible, and has a user-friendly interface. For people and businesses who wish to take blogging seriously, WordPress is the platform of choice.

It has been proved that business owners who blog on Etsy make more sales than those who do not. The higher sales are due to the relationships built with consumers and blog readers, who will continue to purchase in the future. To ensure success for your Etsy shop, keep the following guidelines in mind when blogging:

- Make an effort to be consistent in order to maintain momentum.

- By incorporating others in your blog, you can create a community. Get a large number of individuals to follow the blog's activity on a regular basis.

- Use your blog to further the brand for your Etsy shop and your merchandise. Your blog should essentially be an extension of your brand and a reflection of it.

- A blog should be enjoyable to read. Both the business owner and the readers should have a good time with it. When it stops being enjoyable, the blog may no longer be effective as a marketing tool.

Article Writing

Writing articles with a link back to your website or Etsy shop and submitting them to article directories is referred to as article marketing. There are a lot of article marketing sites or article directories to choose from, so you should be doing some research and find the finest ones. Ezine is the most comprehensive article directory.

Writing articles is a frequently free way that Etsy businesses may utilize to promote their Etsy shop and products. Basically, you can market your business and products by writing anything you can think of. Always remember to provide a hyperlink to your Etsy store so that people may visit the page.

Guest Posting

Guest posting, on the other hand, is the creation of articles or providing opinions on the websites of other Etsy shop owners or news sites. Guest posting allows you to improve your network, gain more notoriety, and broaden your reach by establishing backlinks to your Etsy shop.

Writing for other people in the handmade products community's blogs and websites will help you expand your network and consumer base. It is also a chance to meet other individuals in the homemade community who share your interests.

Guest blogging on Etsy will bring you and your Etsy shop some attention. You can begin to establish a name and expand your fan base by submitting articles on other handcrafted websites and blogs. As a consequence, it suffices to say that the more you write, the more you will be recognized.

Guest posting on a variety of websites offers the benefit of broadening your reach and attracting a diverse range of readers and viewers. Because of your brand's ever-expanding reach, an increasing number of people are exposed to it. The overall result is more traffic and revenues for the Etsy store.

Always keep in mind that building back-links to the business is the most critical aspect of all writing. Make sure you have a way to connect back to your Etsy shop in all three of these methods: blogging, article marketing, and guest posting. A short bio at the conclusion of every article gives you the option of including a backlink. The objective of backlinks is to improve search engine exposure, especially if they come from well-known and high-ranking websites.

SEO or search engine optimization is a strategy for supporting search engines in determining the relevance of a webpage or blog. The focus of an Etsy store owner should be on ensuring that Google, a search engine, knows the type of product they are selling. When building up the Etsy shop, some SEO was integrated in at the time of putting tags. As a response, when people are searching for a specific term associated with your business or product, Google will display you higher in the results list.

OFFER DISCOUNTS

You can also do plenty of marketing by offering sales and discounts at various times. Offering a discount for a specific amount off or a percentage off could be the incentive some buyers need to acquire one of your products. Go to "Marketing" and then "Sales and Coupons" in the Shop Manager. You can run a percent-off sale (between 10% and 70% off) or provide a dollar-off coupon. All coupon names you choose can only be used once.

You can create coupons that are emailed to consumers after they make a purchase or that can be used on current orders if you establish a minimum. Set the minimum higher if you just want to offer a discount on your more expensive items or a group of items. Create a variety of coupons and distribute them in various locations (Instagram, business cards, thank-you emails, etc.) to evaluate which ones are the most beneficial for you. Etsy's marketing tab will show you how well your coupons are selling.

On the other side, offering discounts or sales can make your products appear "cheap" and unappealing to potential purchasers. If you run sales frequently, you may be conditioning your clients to wait to buy since they know there will be another deal shortly. If your things are only selling at a discount, it could indicate that your original price is simply too high. Instead of offering too many discounts or deals, I try to concentrate on my target market and tailor my products and prices accordingly. You will be better able to design products that you know people will like at rates you know they will pay if you can develop a picture of your target market - whether through Facebook insights, market research, or simply seeing who is purchasing your stuff. Yes, creating something that you believe is beautiful is wonderful, but will someone else find it attractive enough to purchase it? You will not need to run several deals to sell stale inventory if you keep your consumers' preferences and budget in mind.

Customers can now receive personalized offers. For example, if a client has left an item in their cart for at least 24 hours (Abandoned Cart Offer), or if a client has favorited one of your items for at least 48 hours (Favorited Item Offer), you can offer them a coupon (Favorited Listings Offer). Etsy will charge you $0.10 for each automated email it sends to these consumers with the coupon code you have created if you create this type of deal.

9. GROWING YOUR ENTERPRISE

Once you've got your shop set up and you've got some regular customers, you might want to think about expanding your enterprise. You don't have to of course, but if you want to take your shop to the next level, there are a lot of ways to do it.

MAINTAIN GOOD CUSTOMER RELATIONS

It's much easier to get a previous customer to come back than to bring in a new one. As such, good and consistent customer relations should always be a top priority to helping your shop grow. After you have designed your products to your greatest abilities and attracted people to your store, it is critical that you provide the best shopping experience possible.

Client service excellence entails presenting your items in an appealing manner, responding to customer concerns and requests, and offering a seamless purchasing experience, which includes timely shipping. Your clients have every right to expect a professional experience while dealing with you. The fact that Etsy store owners are self-employed makes no difference to this assumption. Buyers want to have all the great experiences they have come to anticipate from an Amazon purchase or a trip to the mall.

It is critical to provide excellent customer service. Aside from repeat business, customers are also a source of referrals. Shoppers on Etsy are frequently active members in the Etsy community. They choose their preferred stores, compile shopping lists, and submit product reviews.

A bad experience that leads to a negative review and discourages other potential customers from visiting your store. Remember that you are running a business here. You should always be polite, prompt, and calm. Sloppiness or incompetence will not be tolerated. If you slack off in any way, they will not return.

Respond Promptly to Customers' Questions and Requests

Answering consumers' queries and reacting to their requests is one of the most significant ways you can build relationships with them. You have the ability to respond to a basic question with such warmth that a consumer regards you as trustworthy and reliable right away. That is the kind of customer who returns time and time again.

An online inquiry puts a buyer one step closer to making a purchase. Make sure that the customer does not have to wait too long for a response. You know how it feels to be pushed aside and treated as if you and your inquiry do not matter if you have ever waited in a store to ask a question while the salesperson was on the phone instead of paying attention to you. That is not how you want your consumers to feel. Instead, say, "I am here for you," with your prompt attention and friendly demeanor.

It is also critical to reply to all forms of client communication. Thank your buyer for leaving you a favorable review on Etsy. In addition, if the review is poor, you must rise above your rage or defensiveness. Simply express your gratitude for the comments, state that you value each and every review, and pledge to improve in the future. Your cool demeanor in the face of the unfavorable review may not persuade the disgruntled customer to reconsider, but it will leave a positive impression on future visitors who read it.

Do not leave anything to chance when it comes to consumer satisfaction. Follow up with a visitor to your shop who makes an inquiry but does not make a purchase. If there is anything you can do to help answer a query or provide more information, do so in a courteous manner. Keep in touch with everyone who visits your shop and makes a purchase, everyone is a potential regular client. Make announcements about your new products or send out updates about your shop on a regular basis. You are developing a relationship with your client. Maintaining and nurturing the friendship is entirely up to you.

USING DATA TO EXPAND

The key to data analytics is to take a look back to all your order history. Examine which of your products is a bestseller and you can maybe highlight that listing, so it is the first thing that appears whenever a new customer checks out your shop. We can presume that your best-selling product is good because why else would it be identified as such? Anyway, aside from that, you can also try and give out a feedback form to your previous clients who have successfully transacted with you. Ask them how they found your products or your online store and collate all the responses you will get. Here, you can study the strengths and weaknesses of your marketing strategy. Consider answering the following questions:

- Which social media platform generates the most clicks to my product or store?
- Which one has the least?
- What is the basic demographic of my customer?
- What improvement can I make?
- Do I have to re-profile my target market?

You see, this is just a very simple take on data analytics. You can do this alone when your store is still relatively small but once it grows into a big enterprise, do consider hiring a professional data analyst to do the work for you. There are lots of technicalities in this field that need professional intervention. Also realize that online market is volatile ever since the idea of trendsetting emerged. That is why you may need a professional to keep score of all the changes happening in the business. Of course, this isn't necessary.

CAPITALIZE ON SPECIAL OCCASIONS

Right now, it's holiday season, not only in your country, but all throughout the world, with virtually every day being a holiday. It means that by properly presenting your things and creating holiday specials that you can distribute to various parts of the world, you may make a significant amount of money.

Consider the length of the Diwali vacation, a multi-day festival, and the amount of money you could save by designing specific things with India in mind. Isn't it a good deal? What about Halloween, which takes place in October? The concept of Halloween is to dress up in unusual and unusual costumes. You could make and sell such things.

As an Etsy vendor, what do you need to know? It is a straightforward procedure. All you have to do is use the website's gift feature to assist folks in purchasing exceptional and distinctive gifts for their loved ones. The majority of people from all around the world will be looking for something to give to their loved ones. The main benefit of the Etsy gift function, which was created in 2012 and has helped people who have no idea what to give their loved ones choose extraordinary gifts, is that you may assist individuals who have no idea what they need to offer their loved ones choose wonderful presents.

What are some of the items you would sell on Etsy for a holiday special? There are numerous. Given that most of your things will be handcrafted with love, it is only natural to think that they will all be one-of-a-kind. As a result, anything on Etsy can be sold as a Christmas special with correct packaging.

Jewelry is always desired. A good piece of jewelry will be wrapped attractively and mailed off as a classic present no matter what time of year it is. Some items, on the other hand, are more distinctive. A gift of a customized photo album, for example, would be greatly appreciated by the recipient. What about a maroon pillowcase in the shape of a heart? That, too, would be fantastic.

How about some amusing holiday greeting cards? What about vintage flower vases and antique boxes? Woolen ponchos, enticing African attire, unique beads, ancient metal strands, unique and fragrant soaps prepared at home, and so on. On Etsy, you will find a plethora of holiday-themed items. If you are stumped for holiday ideas, check out the Etsy website to see what other people have come up with. However, keep in mind that the most essential thing here is to pick a gift that will have the most impact on the recipient and that can be utilized for any occasion.

DIVERSIFY YOUR PRODUCT OFFERINGS

When you look at the major details of what is trendy and what is in style, you'll be able to make the best decisions about what you should sell and how to advertise it. As a result, you have to keep an eye on the most important news in your industry and make the appropriate decisions. By doing so, you will be able to improve your company's overall output in the appropriate way, and you will be able to propel your Etsy store to the very top of the business ladder.

Another crucial consideration that will aid you in realizing your ambitions of Etsy dominance is the necessity to refresh your product list on a regular basis. If you do not modify the products you sell, they will get stale in terms of fashion. Everyone is eager for fresh trends and product lines. It does not matter if it is about clothes, jewelry, or anything else. You always need a new wave every now and then. Try to create new things that will catch people's attention and make you appreciate the pleasure they provide.

So go ahead and update the list and make some positive adjustments to your Etsy store. Surprise presents are a great strategy to increase your sales. When you give your consumers a surprise gift, it builds anticipation, which can help you increase your sales. Try to think of the best surprises you can come up with and build tension among your audience. Don't let them down with the unexpected gifts, and attempt to make them pleased with these nice surprises. When consumers are pleased with your small efforts, it will boost your brand's image and even lead to increased sales. There are many different types of surprise presents from which to choose, and you should always attempt to change them a little to keep your clients guessing.

The next thing to consider is whether or not you can add a personal touch to your offering. Keeping track of your customers' birthdays and even anniversaries implies that you may send them a greeting on these special occasions.

These small acts of kindness go a long way toward ensuring that you have a long list of satisfied consumers. They will appreciate the gesture if they receive surprise personal messages on special occasions, and it may encourage them to remain loyal to your brand. Everyone enjoys being treated with respect, and your customers are no exception.

As a result, attempt to keep up with a program that will remind you of these important dates and send out automated emails or even promotional codes to your client list as gifts. Etsy is one such website that is known for offering a variety of unique features. You should attempt to keep a close eye on it at all times because you never know which feature will come in handy. When you look into the specifics of the top features, you will get a better understanding of the important elements, which can help you run your store more efficiently.

So, get ready to investigate the major methods in which you may improve upon the various Etsy features, and then get ready to relish the rewards that it can bring to your store. You should always be aware of what your competitors have to offer, including the types of things they sell and the kind of reviews they receive. In the business world, you must not only provide the greatest products, but you must also ensure that your services are superior to those provided by your competitors. This will make a significant difference and give you a competitive advantage.

You should strive to visit their stores on a regular basis to keep track of the changes they make. You will be able to create a quick notion about how to surpass their popularity if you can figure out and brainstorm the causes for their popularity. This kind of knowledge will enable you to stay ahead of the competition and enjoy Etsy supremacy.

Gaining an advantage over your competition is one of the most wanted abilities that you must possess in order to boost your business production.

Additionally, you must constantly strive to improve your Etsy shop. You should witness positive and influencing adjustments in your Etsy business as long as you are dedicated enough to always seek out to bring in the proper kind of modifications. Your store will not experience any changes if you cease putting in the effort to bring in fresh improvements. This will have an impact on the quantity of profit you will make. When it comes to becoming the most popular Etsy store, there are a slew of factors to consider.

Even if you make the best modifications, your store's growth will level off after a while. The appropriate thing to do is to maintain enhancing the store because your customers will notice the gradual improvements and will remain glued to your store.

Those that aspire to have the best Etsy store must be continually on the lookout for the most innovative ways to keep their shop at the top of the heap.

YOUR COMPANY IN THE LONG RUN

Once the business starts to grow, some of us tend to be complacent. You should unlearn and completely forget about this behavior. The fundamental reason for this is that business requires continuous monitoring and updating.

It is possible that your business will slacken if you do not pay attention to it properly. Even if you put in the correct amount of work, your strategies may not always lead the way to success. The success of your company is sometimes determined by variables other than your strategies. This is why you must monitor the effectiveness of your strategies.

When you keep an eye on the progress meter and regularly monitor the company's growth, you will be able to figure out what works and what does not. It is possible that failing to keep frequent checks can affect your company. You must focus on the dynamics of excellent business tactics if you want your Etsy store to be considered among the greatest in the league.

Some of you might believe that statistics do not always matter, and that numbers do not make a company. Do you have contradictory thoughts? Please allow me to clarify. Have you ever considered the connection between research and business? It should come as no surprise that in order to run a successful business, you must be well-versed in numbers, data, and other factors.

You will have a lot better and clearer understanding of things if you look into the depths of the statistics related to Etsy store, the products they have sold, and the many patterns and styles that are now popular. You will need to extract the correct kind of data if you want to develop your firm. It will not be of assistance until and until you have the information in hand. Managing a business needs a great deal of thought and planning. You will have a lot more points to work on if the research work you have invested for the firm is very strong. This will help you increase your chances of succeeding in your business.

The amount of study that can be done is limitless, and you must be willing to participate in it. Continue to delve further into the intricacies, and then put the information into practice to better your company. You will be more ready to handle the many facets of your business once you have analyzed all of these data.

10. OTHER THINGS TO CONSIDER

T he basic principles of operating and handling a business are simple enough. However, there are always difficulties that are kept less well known and not so often discussed. While you can develop some of your own techniques, there are some strategies and situations we can advise you to avoid.

ALWAYS DOUBLE-CHECK THE DETAILS

This is a common blunder that occurs as a result of a heavy workload and haste. Never deliver a shipment without double-checking the information, especially if your client has left any comments. If you think that a mistake has been made, like a typo for instance, do not hesitate to raise your concern. If something in the order puzzles you, do not be hesitant to ask for confirmation.

It's always fun to sit around with friends and tell tales about someone who purchased a hammer and instead received a pair of scissors. Or how a shipment that was supposed to go to Alaska wound up in Albuquerque. It is only amusing to those who listen to it. It's not so funny to the client who made the error, and it is not amusing to you who may have lost a client as a result of the mistake.

SHIP YOUR ITEMS SMARTLY

The products must be delivered in one piece to their final destination. It would be useless for anyone if a one-of-a-kind vintage item came smashed at its destination. If I ordered a 1957 Fender Precision bass guitar, and it arrived with the neck split from the body, the strings snapped, and the pick guard hanging out of the body, I would be enraged! I would want recompense right away, regardless of who was to blame, especially for a product on which I would have paid thousands of dollars!

This is the point at which we must make a critical observation. According to the law, the company from which the buyer purchased the product, which is you, is liable for such situations. That is to say, if any apologies or compensations are required, they will be paid from your hide!

It is your job to ensure that everything you ship is wrapped properly and with enough precautions to ensure that your product arrives safely at its destination, regardless of what the transportation company does. Never expect that a delivery service will treat your items with care. That is not the case.

MAKE SURE YOUR THINGS ARE NOT UNDERPRICED

This is not just about generating a respectable profit. It's also about not being compensated for the time you spent developing the product. It's a matter of trust, as it is with a few other situations. Low price makes people think its low quality.

Everyone is aware of the amount of effort that goes into a handcrafted item. And everyone appreciates a handcrafted item precisely because it is handcrafted. In a customer's view, this automatically translates to a larger price. Low prices quickly bring to mind things created by machines. This is why they are hesitant to trust a low-cost item.

The most common mistake is to look at what others charge and then charge the same or a bit less. Before deciding on the price's sweet spot that will bring you sales and cash, you must first determine how much you are paying for raw materials, utility costs, and tool replacement.

THINK LIKE A CUSTOMER

You must take a step outside of yourself. When writing descriptions and offering information, the basic rule of thumb is to consider what the people who will be reading them truly want to know. What may appear to you as an obvious element that could be overlooked does not necessarily mean that it is so to others. Every detail matters, and not everyone has the same brain capacity for comprehending subtleties.

If you are selling toys for kids, then imagine yourself as a parent, even if you do not have any of your own. Consider yourself a musician if you are selling musical instruments. Writing those descriptions as yourself is one of the most common blunders you can do, and one you should avoid at all costs. If required, have someone knowledgeable about the product you wish to sell inform you what would be expected to be read in the description and other tags.

STAY AWAY FROM PRODUCTS THAT ARE OBJECTIONABLE

Failure to pay attention to the nature of what they sell is a common mistake that vendors make. Although it may appear harmless to you, it may be offensive to others. The problem doesn't involve any sexually explicit content. It also contains items that have the potential to cause racism, discrimination based on gender or sexual orientation, and religious offenses.

In truth, there is some ambiguity in this situation. What constitutes offensive behavior and what does not? What religious zealots perceive objectionable to their faith may be deemed freedom of speech and expression by others.

You have tremendous control over this situation. Moderation and careful thought are necessary, according to our advice. It is possible that more racy products will sell better. However, they might also exacerbate your difficulties. If you choose to pursue more extreme choices, you should make it clear on your profile so that consumers know what to expect while browsing your products. Negative reviews can be avoided with the help of a relevant caution.

NEVER FAIL TO ANSWER

People will always have questions, no matter how meticulously you prepare your descriptions. As previously stated, various people interpret things in different ways. Many vendors fail to respond to inquiries they consider unimportant or questions that have already been answered during the product presentation. Worse, they react with the lazy and unhelpful phrase "Just read the description."

This is the type of mistake that you should always try to avoid. Sometimes the person asking the inquiry already knows the answer. They might ask it to see if you will answer at all, as well as to assess your level of professionalism. You will lose the customer if you fail to respond or if you reply in a demeaning manner. Make a conscious effort to pay very close attention towards each question and respond immediately.

MAKE YOUR REVIEWS OR RATINGS PUBLIC AT ALL TIMES

People will be checking to check what other people are saying about you and how they regard your manner of doing business unless you are a new seller. Positive reviews are always appreciated, but a well-received critical review might provide even more benefits.

Never underestimate the impact of a positive retort to a bad remark. That is a mistake that is much worse than not replying at all to the unfavorable comment. Although you may be unable to respond to a bad review, you can ensure that it does not occur again.

THE SELLER PROTECTION PROGRAM IS NOT TO BE OVERLOOKED

There will be issues with your financial transactions from time to time. It makes no difference who is to blame. What is important is that if you do not use this protection, the error will show up in your account's status, and the ramifications could be severe.

THE LEGALITIES OF ETSY

After you have decided on a business name, check with your city/county officials to determine if you will need a business license. In many jurisdictions, a business license is a one-time fee based on your company's annual gross sales, and it is a small but necessary cost to do business. Scam websites, particularly those that need money in order to locate the forms you seek, should be avoided. A quick Google search will almost always bring up scam sites first, so check for sites that come from your city or county, or simply visit the Commissioner of Revenue, Treasurer, or Clerk of Court in your city or county.

Taxes and Other Fees

Nobody likes thinking about taxes, but they're an important consideration if you want to be serious about selling your product online. Naturally, the taxes you have to pay are different depending on where you are and your nationality.

To have access to things like business bank accounts, business insurance, and so on, certain provinces may need you to register your business name (which can be a unique company name or your personal name). Every area conducts business registration differently, so be sure to look up your own specific situation.

Keep in mind that Etsy will normally convert fees incurred in US Dollars on these reports, so double-check that you are monitoring everything in your local currency since anything that goes on your tax return has to be reported in such.

If you live in the United States and your state requires it, contact the tax agency, and register to collect sales tax once you have your company license. Only charge and collect sales tax on things shipped within your state or things purchased from you within your state (local pickup, craft fair, etc.). You must determine if your state is a source or a destination of sales tax. If your state is a sales tax originating state, you will be charged sales tax at the rate in effect where you are. If your state is a sales tax destination state, you will have to charge tax depending on the location of the customer, which could require keeping track of a variety of different tax rates.

You can also purchase wholesale and tax-free items (for resale) with your sales tax ID. Each merchant has their own procedure, but you will almost always need to produce your sales tax number, as well as a copy of your tax-exempt form. Wholesaling and purchasing tax-free will save you a good amount of money! If you pay sales tax on the goods you buy to use in your resale items for any reason, you must still charge sales tax if the item is shipped to a consumer in the state. To put it another way, just because you had to pay sales tax doesn't necessarily mean you should not pass it along to your customers. If you opt not to apply for a business license or a sales tax ID (where applicable), you risk getting found and paying hefty fines in the future. Etsy does not need you to supply your sales tax ID, but depending on your sales volume, they may need your Federal ID or social security number.

If you live in a member nation of the European Union, you should be aware that Etsy will withhold the sums related to the Value Added Tax that applies to all member states and send it to the proper tax authorities in your name. This means you may not have to do anything to report this money to the proper tax authorities, but you will have to report the income from your Etsy shop sales.

THE CHALLENGES OF ETSY

Since its debut, Etsy has accumulated more than 4.3 million people selling their crafts worldwide. The majority of these sellers are women who sell their products from home. That seems like good news, doesn't it? However, if all of the businesses were equally successful, then there would be millions more female millionaires in the world today.

But it isn't really like that, is it? There are a lot of nuances involved in developing a successful Etsy store, and your product's quality alone is not enough to entice customers.

A high level of competition. On the other side, you are going into a marketplace where there are over 30 million consumers interested in arts and crafts. Conversely, there are nearly 2 million different retail locations in operation. It will be difficult to stand out in this extremely competitive landscape. This is where the act of being genuine comes into play. Several merchants on Etsy have acquired a distinct appearance over time, and products with the same design tend to look similar as well. Before getting too involved, make sure you fully understand the work you want to get done and the audience you want to satisfy.

In order to finalize a sale, a buyer will place an order on your ad, and you just send the product. This is a no-brainer, isn't it? If that is so, why are so many Etsy shops failing, and why does getting customers seem to be such a challenge?

This is where you have to think about everything that comes on behind the scenes of running a shop. It's important to take into account overhead and backend costs as well as how to increase sales efficiency. Anyone who would not want all of their orders neatly put out, with money already paid, and shipping addresses ready for delivery has probably lost their marbles.

Like any other store, whether it's brick-and-mortar or online, selling on Etsy requires the right amount of work, attention, and dedication to find success. You'll get what you put into the venture. If you're ready to spend time on the project then you'll go far. But don't take the decision lightly! Quality customer service is especially vital, given the high competition and the plethora of other small businesses a consumer may visit if they are not satisfied. And in order to make sure that all of your shipments are done on schedule, you will have to build listings that are highly optimized and make sure your sales are monitored. However, that's where this guide comes in to help explain.

CONCLUSION

There are a so many great reasons why you might want to start your own Etsy shop. It does not matter if you're doing it for personal reasons, professional reasons, or anything else. At the same time, you can choose to sell things there casually as a hobby, or choose to turn it into a business.

If you are one of these people, and you have carefully read what you need to know and what you need to do, and you have determined that creating a store using Etsy's platform is the best option for you, all we can say is "welcome to the world of Etsy."

Etsy was founded with the goal of allowing shoppers to purchase things directly from the people who develop and manufacture them. They offer one-of-a-kind and vintage items, as well as giving merchants access to a far broader audience and market than regular craft fairs. There, customers can find goods from all over the world that they would not otherwise be able to at local shops. And on the other side of things, sellers can start their own business on Etsy's platform with minimal effort and by utilizing the resources that Etsy gives for this reason.

For you as a sellers, starting a shop on Etsy is a reasonably simple process overall that can provide results if you have the patience and determination. You can succeed if you use some very simple ideas and approaches that have been time tried for their efficiency, while avoiding the traps and common blunders that come with it. A person who wants to open a traditional brick and mortar shop will need a lot of money or enough financing to cover the costs of the rent, the initial equipment, the advertisement, the Internet site, the proper arrangements to comply with the relevant law's safety and security regulations, the initial stock, and enough money to last until the next payday. However, when you decide to build an e-store rather inside, your overhead costs reduce dramatically. If you who will develop and bring the Internet site to life, it will still require funds, but you'll be able to turn a profit much quicker. And if you want to expand you Etsy store into something larger you can. You can choose to expand your hobby into a business and run it as long as possible if you want. What you do and how much energy you put into it is up to you!

No matter what your goals on Etsy are, hopefully you'll have a good idea of what you can do on this site after reading this. As a result, you know how to successfully establish an Etsy store. While this is only the beginning of your journey, the work will certainly keep you busy for a long time. If you made a high-quality product and put your whole heart and all of your imagination into developing something exceptional for your clients, you should give it as many opportunities as possible for success.

Made in United States
North Haven, CT
30 April 2023